...el genesi...
...n mos...
...e Lanim...

...libro de los vivientes, pio
que sin mas dilatarlo
...ruina inspiracion movido
...angel, y ansi se lebantoa
a leyendo, y demandaaun
vnas tixeras ~~bien dichas~~,
y se fue sobre la barranca
...cia, y encendido deseo deser
...neste sacram. s. es imposs.
...i todo el prepucio, de mane

...fue
...tos, y
...los tra
...a pues
...hores
...recibio
...tima
al. ..m
y alab

THE

RETURN OF

CARVAJAL

A Mystery

Ilan Stavans

Etchings by Eko

The Pennsylvania State University Press
University Park, Pennsylvania

The frontispiece and last page of this volume reproduce the
first and last pages of the Luis de Carvajal manuscripts gathered
in one volume (including his autobiography, principles of faith,
Ten Commandments, and a prayer manual). Digital images appear
by permission of the Princeton University Library.

Cataloging-in-publication data is on file with the Library of
Congress. ISBN 978-0-271-08470-1 (hardcover)

The Pennsylvania State University Press is a member of the
Association of University Presses.

It is the policy of The Pennsylvania State University Press to use
acid-free paper. Publications on uncoated stock satisfy the minimum
requirements of American National Standard for Information
Sciences—Permanence of Paper for Printed Library Material,
ANSI Z39.48–1992.

To Oliver Sacks (1933–2015)
& Martín F. Yiriart (1942–2013)

Books are not made to be believed, but to be subjected to inquiry.

When we consider a book, we mustn't ask ourselves what it says but what it means.

—**Umberto Eco**
The Name of the Rose (1980)

Contents

List of Illustrations viii

Part I: Lost

1. The Thief 3
2. The Prophet 25

Part II: Found

3. The Chronicler 49
4. The Collector 71

Notes 89

Illustrations

1. Eko, *Plaza del Quemadero*, 2019   2

2. Eko, *The Thief*, 2019   11

3. Eko, *The Manuscript*, 2019   16

4. Eko, *Luis de Carvajal the Elder*, 2019   24

5. Eko, *The Apocalypse of Ezra*, 2019   31

6. Eko, *Isabel de Carvajal*, 2019   37

7. Eko, *The Arrest*, 2019   40

8. Eko, *Ilan Stavans*, 2019   48

9. Eko, *Santa Inquisición*, 2019   53

10. Eko, *Anita Brenner*, 2019   56

11. Eko, *Nueva España*, 2019   64

12. Eko, *The Collectors*, 2019   70

13. Eko, *Auto-da-Fé*, 2019   79

14. Eko, *The Martyr*, 2019   84

Part I Lost

Whoever destroys a soul,
it is considered as if he
destroyed an entire world.

—*Talmud Yerushalmi*
Sanhedrin 4:1 (22a)

The Thief

The sudden reemergence of a misplaced item is often a stroke of luck. We lose a set of keys, a watch, a phone, or a photograph, and then, without fanfare, it shows up again. That's because nothing really disappears; it is just hidden from sight. Losing things is part of being alive. And finding them, too.

However, when it comes to a long-lost book of historical relevance, whose value accrues as time goes by, its reappearance can be, in truth, less serendipitous than it may seem. Often, it abruptly gets rediscovered because there is a new context for it. Those who had lost it, as well as those who had frantically pursued it, are long gone, and with them the original reasons for the disappearance. But the moment that fresh context sets in, there are new reasons to find it. And then, out of the blue, it pops up.

What actually occurs is that people are unknowingly waiting for it. And so it arrives, unheralded yet ready to test long-standing assumptions.

This is what happened with the Carvajal booklet. Strictly speaking, its disappearance wasn't shocking. To this day, the Archivo General de la Nación is far from a tightly controlled environment. Mexican libraries in general aren't known for their security or efficiency, and the Archivo, Mexico's national archive, conducts business in a similarly relaxed manner. Manuscripts, books, magazines, newspapers, and other materials are often misplaced or go missing. Staff members are not always well trained. They belong to a labor union notorious for its allergy to any type of personnel improvement. All of this explains how walking out with a manuscript from its facilities is not difficult to imagine: you request a book, you sit in the rare books room for a while pretending to read it, you put it in your handbag, and you leave the premises. You will pass as unnoticed as a fly on the wall.

In 1932, when the Carvajal booklet—a relatively small item, roughly 4 by 3 inches, about the size of an adult hand—vanished from the Archivo, the security was even more lax, if that is possible.

A decade earlier, Mexico had gone through a bloody civil war, La Revolución Mexicana, that left an estimated one million people dead. It was Mexico's first such armed struggle of the twentieth century. It coincided with the First World War in Europe. The Bolshevik upheaval was still in the future. Though the war began in 1910, its aftermath lingered well into the late 1920s, when a single ruling party, the PRI (Partido Revolucionario Institucional), took hold of power and didn't relinquish it for more than seventy years.

In the midst of this massive national reconstruction, keeping track of an artifact like this little booklet would have been far from people's attention. The collective drive was devoted to modernizing

Mexico. *Mestizaje*, the mix of European and indigenous traits, hardened into an ideology. Unlike the United States, which at the time was a young, forward-looking empire setting new global rules, the emerging Mexican nation was intent on emphasizing its Aztec past, which it sought to portray in homogeneous ways. Amidst these cultural convulsions, the chronicle of a crypto-Jew coming to terms with his lapsed Mosaic faith was by no means a priority.

The Archivo also contained some 1,550 volumes with *procesos* and other proceedings of the Inquisition. None garnered a great deal of interest. For anyone with even a small knowledge of Jewish history in the New World, however, the volume in question—a 180-page manuscript handwritten by a crypto-Jew targeted by the Holy Office of the Inquisition for unlawful proselytizing activities—was not only distinct but enormously valuable. The author's name was Luis de Carvajal *el Mozo* (meaning the Younger), a sobriquet that distinguished him from his famous uncle, Luis de Carvajal y de la Cueva, aka *el Viejo* (the Elder), who was governor of the northern Mexican region of Nuevo León and had a reputation for dealing diplomatically with the indigenous population of the area.[1] (The younger Carvajal had other appellations, too, including the Hebrew name Joseph Lumbroso, borrowed from the biblical character Joseph.[2])

Carvajal composed the biographical manuscript that would end up in the Archivo just before the tragic end of his life. On 8 December 1596, at the age of thirty, he was burned at the stake in what was arguably the biggest auto-da-fé ever in New Spain, as Mexico was then known. It might also have been the most ostentatious auto-da-fé in all of Latin America. The volume in question recounts Carvajal's rediscovery of his Jewishness after having been raised a Catholic in Spain—and tells how he came to recognize himself as a messiah for other crypto-Jews who lived far away from the Iberian Peninsula, where the Spanish Inquisition exercised its might.

Although public executions under the Spanish Inquisition have attracted substantial attention, the truth is that very few took place.[3] In essence, an auto-da-fé is a judicial court that takes the form of a theatrical performance. Dressed in a variety of *sanbenitos* (atoning garments), and having already been tortured to confess and provide names of other *judaizantes* (Judaizers), victims were paraded in front of large audiences until they reached the Plaza Mayor, today's Plaza del Quemadero, the Burning Plaza, in downtown Mexico City. That ominous December day, from 9:30 A.M. until 2:00 P.M., Carvajal had been put on the rack and denounced by 121 people, including some of his relatives. During the actual immolation, he had stood next to his mother, Leonor Carvajal, and one of his sisters, Isabel Carvajal, all of them accused by the colonial branch of the Inquisition.

What they said to one another is not known. We have a few surviving pictorial representations of the auto-da-fé. Judging from them, bystanders must have been transfixed as the fire devoured the fleeting bodies. The Catholic Church wanted to create a scene that would serve as a warning to the population. Carvajal was a sinner. Aberrant people like him would burn in hell. The Inquisition was simply making that punishment tangible on this earth.

Did Carvajal actually repent in front of his inquisitors? At first, he did, and then he recanted. But it doesn't matter. Toward the end of his life, self-preservation was not his aim: he undoubtedly wanted his death to be a sacrifice.

The booklet was intended for his siblings. It included an autobiographical meditation that fills out the bulk of it. (That section is sometimes referred to as Carvajal's "Last Will and Testament.") In the back, it also had prayers and scriptural selections, including a transcription of the Ten Commandments as well as of Maimonides's Thirteen Principles of Faith, which are included in every Jewish prayer book and are recited as a liturgical hymn at the conclusion of a Friday or holiday Jewish service. The recitation is known as the *Yigdal*. It represents the fundamental pillars of Judaism, to which crypto-Jews in the New World didn't have easy access.

Carvajal acknowledges that no matter how much he would be tortured, his role in this life was to become a martyr. Suffering was a way to justify his mission. It gave him gravitas.

In Mexico and Peru, the two centers of the Holy Office of the Inquisition in the Spanish- and Portuguese-speaking Americas, the total number of prosecutions was considerably smaller than in Spain, where the office was founded in 1478. Indeed, among *conversos*, as New Christians in the Iberian Peninsula and elsewhere were sometimes known, the so-called Nuevo Mundo was seen as a safe haven of sorts.[4] Not that persecution was altogether absent; it simply took place farther away. In the Kingdom of Castile, the Inquisition had headquarters in Seville, Toledo, Valladolid, and Granada, among other places. The Inquisition in Mexico was established in 1570 and lasted until 1820, a decade after the nation became independent. Historians believe that about 325 people were persecuted by the Inquisition in Mexico for being Jewish, and approximately 30 were executed as

judaizantes. Carvajal is the most famous among them.

As it became independent and its institutions began to flourish, Mexico sought to safeguard its past in institutions devoted to recording various aspects of daily life. The Carvajal booklet was part of the inquisitorial *procesos* that ended up at the Archivo. It was the natural place for them, for the Archivo also holds other national treasures: signed documents dating back to the movement for independence from Spain in 1810, correspondence between political leaders of the nineteenth century, court proceedings, various drafts of the nation's constitution and its amendments, and so on.

Before the Carvajal booklet disappeared from the Archivo, we know for sure that a transcription of it was made. Various scholars, such as Seymour B. Liebman, the author of three important resources on Mexico's colonial period—*The Enlightened* (1967), which is about Carvajal; *The Jews in New Spain* (1970); and *New World Jewry, 1493–1825: Requiem for the Forgotten* (1982)—say that they used it in their research. A transcription was also the basis of a couple of English translations.

Carvajal's memoir was probably written between 1591 and 1592, after he was arrested the first of two times by the Inquisition. His crime: "unlawful activities," that is, behavior that inspired others in Mexico City and other parts of the country to return to Judaism. What's most striking about the narrative is that it is written in the third person. That is, Carvajal looks at himself from a distance, as a character. The memoir portrays the way he discovered his heritage and used it as a coalescing force for the adrift souls of crypto-Jews. At one point he talks of going, as an adult, with an acquaintance to the banks of the Pánuco River in order to circumcise himself. The ceremony is seen as a seal of covenant: Carvajal was born in the wilderness because his family was forced to renounce its Judaism, and through the circumcision, he is back among the tribe.

When I read the story for the first time, in my twenties, I was mesmerized. The fact that the Carvajal family had kept its faith a secret for almost a century seemed astounding. In the early 1980s, Mexican Jews had little interest in religion. We were culturally Jewish, which meant merely that our sensibility was part of a long chain of generations. We absorbed our Jewishness through language—through readings and movies and music. The rituals and theological convictions seemed secondary. In fact, many of my school friends didn't seem to care too much that they were Jewish. It was an assortment of mundane routines, not an organizing creed.

Carvajal, in contrast, was convinced that faith was his salvation. He refused to allow the political environment to dictate his beliefs. In fact, he was ready to persuade other covert Jews that it was time to return to their ancient practices. I admired that conviction. There was something heroic in it. Not surprisingly, over the centuries scholars have looked at him with similar admiration. In *Los primeros mexicanos: La vida criolla en el siglo XVI* (The first Mexicans: Creole life in the sixteenth century, 1962), Fernando Benítez, one of the most distinguished

Mexican historians, described Carvajal as "the most . . . exciting character in New Spain." According to David M. Szewczyk of The Philadelphia Rare Books & Manuscripts Company, the Carvajal booklet is "the earliest surviving personal narrative by a New World Jew and the earliest surviving worship manuscript and account of coming to the New World."

The first news we have of the booklet's twentieth-century theft appears in Alfonso del Toro's two-volume *The Carvajal Family* (1944), a full-fledged biography not only of Luis de Carvajal but of his entire family: his uncle, his mother, his sister, and other relatives. For del Toro, the Carvajal family was fascinating as a group, not simply as a gathering of individuals. His book is a difficult read, however. Del Toro was not a historian per se but an Archivo employee, and he had done the groundwork for *The Carvajal Family* almost two decades before its publication. It is shot through with racist opinions about *mestizos* and strong anti-Semitic views.[5]

The Carvajal booklet left the Archivo around the time del Toro had begun his research. Years before

his biography of the Carvajal family, he published an edited volume that was part of a series released under the institution's imprimatur. It was called *Los judíos de la Nueva España* (The Jews of New Spain), with a section devoted to Carvajal. Five years later, a volume called *Alumbrado* (Enlightened, 1937), by Pablo Martinez del Río, featured Carvajal's entire proceso—and failed to acknowledge del Toro's earlier contribution. The omission might have been due to carelessness. In any case, the slap in the face spurred del Toro to pursue an even larger project, where his name could appear prominently. That project, which ended up taking him almost a decade, was his magnum opus: the seven-hundred-plus-page portrait of the Carvajal clan.

The Carvajal Family isn't a balanced book. Del Toro's knowledge of Hebrew was nonexistent. His tale is incoherent in parts; he invents information; he occasionally allows his anti-Semitic views to seep into the narrative. But what's pertinent here is that in the introduction to his book, del Toro mentions a rival in the study of Carvajal who apparently walked away from the premises with Carvajal's oeuvre—his memoir and correspondence. It sounds as though del Toro is talking about a thief. But the reader might also sense a hint of jealousy on del Toro's part toward a rival academic, perhaps better trained, with whom he is competing.

That rival was Jacob Nachbin. Born in 1896, he is a mysterious character in this story. He was a Yiddish-speaking *shtetl* orphan from Poland who taught at Northwestern University, in Evanston, Illinois, and at the University of New Mexico in Las Vegas. By all accounts Jacob Nachbin—he also went by the alias Jacques Nachbin—was interested in Sephardic civilization. I have come across various Yiddish publications he authored, including *Der letster fun di groyse Zakutos* (The last of the great Zakutos, 1929), about the last in the dynasty of descendants of Abraham ben Samuel Zacuto, the fifteenth-century mathematician who served as an astronomer in the court of Portugal's King João II.

Almost a century has gone by since Nachbin was active as a scholar, making his whereabouts at various junctures difficult to trace. There a few references to him as a historian of early Jewish life in Brazil. Curiously, he appears to be loosely connected with another major personality in Jewish Latin American letters: the Brazilian author Clarice Lispector, whose extraordinary work is regularly compared to that of Virginia Woolf. Lispector's biographer is Benjamin Moser, whose grandmother was Nachbin's doctoral advisee in Las Vegas. She eventually married him in 1928. (Moser's biography of Lispector includes a footnote that features this information. Nothing more about it is said.)

We know that at some point Nachbin became riveted by Carvajal. He traveled to Mexico City to conduct research at the Archivo, though the exact nature of his project is unknown. According to del Toro, however, it was while Nachbin was studying the memoir that he walked away with it and several other items penned by Carvajal. Del Toro called the authorities, who arrested Nachbin. Del Toro says that Nachbin promised to return the items by mail, but the memoir and a couple of devotional transcriptions vanished into thin air.

Every single one of the participants in this affair is dead. There are no other written accounts of what happened. Still, we need not take del Toro's account at face value. An alternative hypothesis about the robbery could be ventured: namely, that del Toro himself was the thief. In this scenario, the future author of *The Carvajal Family*, who by all accounts appears to have been a jealous type, blamed Nachbin in order to halt his rival's competing research. That would allow del Toro to go solo in pursuit of Carvajal's story.

Either way, the precious booklet, a memoir written in artfully crafted correspondence by Carvajal, went missing from the Archivo in 1932. As news spread, it became an object of intense obsession. Theories abounded about the whereabouts of the Carvajal item: that it was lost in a fire; that it had been returned to the Archivo via Mexican mail (itself a form of purgatory); that a hapless staffer had fatefully placed it in the wrong box; that it lay hidden somewhere in Recife, Brazil, where Nachbin had taken it in a rush to escape the authorities; or that it had fallen into the hands of an unwitting owner in the United Kingdom, who, oblivious to its historical relevance, had consigned it to an attic to accumulate dust.

Although he always claimed that he was innocent, Nachbin was imprisoned in Mexico. He was later extradited, along with his wife, to the United States. The scandal was covered by the Mexican press as well as by Yiddish newspapers in Buenos Aires, at the time the center of Yiddish intellectual culture in the Americas. Those reports were read throughout the Yiddish-speaking world in Latin America, including in Recife, the seafront capital in Brazil's northwestern state of Pernambuco. And in Recife, another of Nachbin's wives, Léa Drechter, an Austrian Jew whom he had abandoned along with their child, learned about the robbery and his bigamy in one fell swoop. (Nachbin had left her and gone to Chicago, where he had reinvented himself as an academic.)

Intriguingly, Nachbin's child, Leopoldo Nachbin, ended up becoming Brazil's most renowned mathematician. He was a childhood friend of Lispector's and appears in a chronicle called "As Grandes Punições" (The great punishments) she wrote in 1967 for *Jornal do Brasil*. In 1948, he went to study under Laurent Schwartz at the University of Chicago, the same city where his father, Jacob Nachbin, had taught more than a decade earlier. Leopoldo Nachbin is internationally known for Nachbin's theorem, a linchpin in complex analysis.

As this tangle of biographical details suggests, the disappearance of the Carvajal booklet inaugurated a decades-long pursuit that involved impostors, polygamists, and pseudo-messiahs, dueling scholars struggling to ensure that their version of events would be engraved in the annals of history, and wealthy philanthropists eager to make sure that old Jewish books still speak to a present awash in anti-Semitic tides. The international curiosity grew so intense that at one point, the booklet at the center of the hunt was described—in reference to the sought-after yet elusive item in Dashiell Hammett's novel—as a Maltese Falcon.

The Prophet

Luis de Carvajal the Younger had been raised with the belief that his family was of Old Christian stock. He was born in Benavente, in northwestern Spain, in 1566 as Luis Rodríguez Carvajal. He traveled to what would become Mexico (he calls it "Occidental India") at the age of fourteen with his family, including his maternal uncle, Luis de Carvajal the Elder.[1] The uncle had been to Mexico once before and was seen as a legendary leader who had helped "pacify the Indians" in the northern territories. For his actions he was named governor of the New Kingdom of León, which is roughly today's state of Nuevo León. Luis de Carvajal the Younger often dropped the "Rodríguez" from his name, emphasizing the maternal side of the family, probably because of his uncle's prominence.

Just before the family sailed across the Atlantic, Carvajal's brother Baltasar delivered a shocking piece of news: the family was New Christian. Furthermore, they secretly practiced Jewish rituals at home, away from the public eye. Baltasar conveyed the news on a particular occasion: he chose Yom Kippur as the date. From then on, Carvajal acknowledged his identity. Carvajal the Elder may have encouraged his family to travel with him with the promise that life in the Spanish colony would allow them to practice their secret religion, if not openly, then at least in a somewhat more relaxed fashion.

The family arrived in Nuevo León in 1580. Carvajal, still a teen, became a businessman, traveling across mining towns and possibly benefiting from the slave trade. At least one slave participated in the conquest of the Aztec capital, Tenochtitlán; others were involved in expeditions, as recounted in Álvar Núñez Cabeza de Vaca's *Chronicle of the Narváez Expedition* (1542). According to some historians, about 200,000 slaves were brought to Mexico during the colonial period.

Five years into Carvajal's life in the New World, during a trip to Mexico City, his father, Francisco Rodríguez, became ill. In the days before Rodríguez died, he told Carvajal all about the family's past and taught him some Jewish practices directly. The memoir implies that the father encouraged his son to become a leader of the crypto-Jewish community in New Spain. Of course, as with all memoirs, Carvajal's is not an objective source; it is full of imaginary sightings and other inventions.

The most dependable study of Carvajal's ordeal is Martin A. Cohen's *The Martyr: Luis de Carvajal, a Secret Jew in Sixteenth-Century Mexico* (1973), which would serve as the source material for an opera that premiered at the San Diego Opera in 1997. Cohen himself enjoyed a colorful biographical background. A Philadelphia native, he taught at the University of Pennsylvania and then joined the US Air Force in 1951. He was ordained as a rabbi in 1957 and became a professor of Jewish history at Hebrew Union College in New York, where he specialized in Sephardic culture in the Americas and traced the relationship between early Christianity and rabbinical Judaism.

The Martyr includes maps and illustrations of the coat of arms and the seal of the Inquisition in Mexico, instruments of torture like the garroting apparatus, the signature of Governor Luis de Carvajal y de la Cueva, letters from Carvajal along with a couple of pages of the "Last Will and Testament," and lithographs depicting interrogations and autos-da-fé from a volume called *El libro rojo, 1520–1867* (The red book, 1520–1867 [1870]), edited by Vicente Riva Palacio and Rafael Payno. Cohen worked on *The Martyr* at the Archivo and in a number of other research institutions. His view of Carvajal was of a "sensitive lad, emotional, volatile, rigid. He could as easily betray as defend someone close to him."[2]

Carvajal's life was full of adventure: his experiences included near misses in his escape from the ubiquitous eyes of the Church, tropical storms en route to the New World, a botched circumcision that amounted to painful self-mutilation, public duels with monks on issues of faith and salvation, and mental illnesses among several family members. In my view, he suffered from delusional outbursts. The memoir repeatedly gives the impression that Carvajal sees himself as a prophet. The story of Joseph—his relationship with his siblings, his unsuspecting journey to Egypt, his prophetic talents, and his closeness with Pharaoh—mesmerized him. Carvajal returns to it repeatedly in his memoir. Following Joseph's example, his martyrdom, as he put it, wasn't a personal choice but part of a cosmic design. He needed to contend with divine revelation, which helps explain his path to immolation.

While the status of crypto-Jews was in itself perilous, Carvajal, I believe, was likely schizophrenic. His schizophrenia is at the base of his messianic drive and fueled his ecstatic visions. Carvajal modeled himself as a spokesperson for divine providence. "What rich and holy palaces you shall see," he chants while in the act of reaching divine communion (as noted above, he always spoke of himself in the third person). "What delightful gardens [there will be] in that Paradise where stands the Tree of Life, a life of bliss everlasting, which will be yours to enjoy!" He labels his eating "supreme holiness at the table of your true Father, who gave you life in this nether world."[3]

With his self-designed conversion to the family's original former faith tradition, which they had been forced to renounce in Spain in the fifteenth century, Carvajal became increasingly open about his Judaism. Granted, what he considered Judaism was really a hodgepodge of idées fixes, stereotypes, and derived knowledge. His quotations from the Hebrew Bible are choppy, selective, and unquestionably filtered through the prism of the New Testament. Cohen believes that Carvajal used the Vulgate as his source. He and other judaizantes in Mexico "didn't discriminate between the Apocrypha and the Old Testament. They realized that the New Testament was unacceptable to Jews, but were unaware that the Apocrypha enjoyed no canonicity

among them." Carvajal doesn't know the full extent of the Jewish calendar. He conflates some holidays and has limited information about others, and he speaks of certain fast days but actually fasts on others.

All this must be seen against the background of crypto-Jewish practices in the New World. When reverting to old family ways, secret Jews often butchered aspects of ritual that had come to them through hearsay. In this respect, the performance of rituals was less a reawakening than an improvisation. Needless to say, after generations of half-remembered loyalties, there could be no easy return to a pristine Judaism. In hindsight, Carvajal looks more like a jazzy mystic and fortune-teller than a sage steeped in rabbinical texts.

In the next few years, Carvajal spent time on an expedition with his uncle to the land of the Chichimecas, a term used by the Aztec people to refer to seminomadic tribes that were rowdy, impatient, and resistant to Aztec customs. These were the unruly "Indians" Carvajal's uncle became famous for appeasing.⁴ It was during this period that Carvajal became infatuated with the book of 2 Esdras, known as the Apocalypse of Ezra, in which he saw the deceit of New Christians and the sacrifice of crypto-Jews as part of a divine plan. Specifically, he heard his calling in 2 Esdras 2 (from the New Revised Standard Version):

¹Thus says the Lord: I brought this people out of bondage, and I gave them commandments through my servants the prophets; but they would not listen to them, and made my counsels void. ²The mother who bore them says to them, "Go, my children, because I am a widow and forsaken. ³I brought you up with gladness; but with mourning and sorrow I have lost you, because you have sinned before the Lord God and have done what is evil in my sight. ⁴But now what can I do for you? For I am a widow and forsaken. Go, my children, and ask for mercy from the Lord." ⁵Now I call upon you, father, as a witness in addition to the mother

of the children, because they would not keep my covenant, ⁶so that you may bring confusion on them and bring their mother to ruin, so that they may have no offspring. ⁷Let them be scattered among the nations; let their names be blotted out from the earth, because they have despised my covenant.

Carvajal increasingly became a vocal leader of those crypto-Jews in New Spain and gave Bible lessons. He continued working as a merchant and even fantasized about escaping, along with some of his followers, to some parts of Europe where religious tolerance was more widely practiced.

His life has a cinematic quality. The memoir, the letters he left behind, and a few messages he wrote during his imprisonment—almost telegraphic, Twitter-like—are, in and of themselves, the stuff of myth. We also have transcriptions of Carvajal's interrogation sessions, which were recorded by his captors. The sessions were brutal exercises in torture. Toward the end, Carvajal struggles to stay on course, describing his own path as consistently as possible while refusing to implicate his relatives, until he breaks and makes a broader confession. The interrogations are reminiscent of those endured by Giordano Bruno and other famous martyrs of the Inquisition. One of the transcriptions, in which Carvajal is in front of his tormentors, reads:

Q. Do your mother and sisters observe the Mosaic Law?

A. No, they have not since they were reconciled in this Holy Office.

Q. What faith do your mother and sisters observe?

A. They observe the faith of Jesus Christ.

Q. How do you know they observe the faith of Jesus Christ?

A. Because they do what the faith of Jesus Christ demands in word and deed.

Q. Since you observe the Law of Moses and preserve it in its belief and believe that you will find salvation in it and no one can be saved through the faith of Jesus Christ, and since you understood, as you do, that they would be damned if they observed the faith of Jesus Christ, how is it that you did not teach your mother and sisters the said Law of Moses?

A. I did not dare because I was very much afraid that one of them might expose me and that I would be arrested by the Holy Office.

Q. This is not credible, because . . . you taught the Law of Moses to strangers, and the Holy Office has sufficient evidence for all of this. You did this because you were driven by the desire for the salvation of the people you taught it to, without regard to the fear that they could denounce you and with unalloyed zeal to spread the Law of Moses and extend its belief. It is clear that if you trusted strangers, you could better trust your mother and sisters, since the love for their own flesh and blood would restrain them from denouncing you to the Holy Office. By the same token you had a greater obligation to look after their salvation and welfare than that of strangers.

A. What you said is the truth.

The Inquisition arrested Carvajal for the first time in 1589, along with his mother and sister. In prison he was paired with a Franciscan monk, whom he ended up successfully converting to Judaism. He heard voices and had visions and prophetic dreams that offered him consolation. In one of these dreams, he was told that "the saints, Job and Jeremiah, are praying for you most efficaciously." It is here that he embraced the identity of the biblical Joseph and adopted the name "Lumbroso." Cohen offers an exposition of Carvajal's thinking: "In his people's Egypt, he was a Joseph, appointed to bring them sustenance in the days of spiritual famine that would precede their miraculous deliverance." Carvajal states that "to practice Judaism is not heresy: It is the will of the Lord our God."

Carvajal was put on trial and sentenced to serve in a hospital in Mexico City; from there, he was later transferred to one of the many schools dedicated to indoctrinating the indigenous population. Once there, he illicitly used the key to the school rector's library to read an assortment of books. The school was not, however, a prison. Carvajal, his mother, and his sister were allowed to spend time at home. Whereas the latter two decided to return to Christianity after their confinement, Carvajal became further radicalized as an adamant Jewish proselytizer. He was furious at his mother and sister and tried to reignite their loyalty to the Hebrew faith.

It is no surprise, then, that in 1595 Carvajal was again under arrest. Carvajal was imprisoned this time after Manuel Lucena, a Portuguese crypto-Jew, denounced him and others in New Spain. The role of inquisitor was shared by Alonso de Peralta, who, according to Seymour B. Liebman, was known for his "stern and frightening" demeanor. The prison warden found, among Carvajal's belongings, three forbidden items written in Latin: Salmorum, Prophete, and Genesis. As a strategy to make him confess, another prisoner was thrown into his cell. That prisoner was really a disguised Dominican cleric called Luis Díaz.

Díaz convinced Carvajal that he was about to be released. Carvajal fell into the trap. He tried to

convert Díaz to Judaism. He told him all sorts of secrets, among them the fact that between his first and second arrest he had written a memoir. He said he had hidden it at his house, in a crack on the wall, and that he hoped that his brothers Miguel and Baltasar would find it and that it would be a tool of resistance for other crypto-Jews. Díaz soon told the guards, and the booklet was confiscated. Its contents were used to incriminate Carvajal, and his relatives were soon imprisoned, too, in the same facility.

Betrayed by the Dominican cleric, and aware that his memoir was now in the hands of his victimizers, a penitent Carvajal resigned himself to his fate. The guards made it known that his mother and sister were now in nearby cells. His ensuing attempts to communicate with his family inject an added dose of pathos of the story.

Feigning lack of hunger, Carvajal declined to eat the food that his captors brought to his cell. He would inscribe short messages in fruit peels or hide them on paper that the inquisitors had left in his cell. He would then ask the guards to bring the food to his relatives.

Needless to say, Carvajal's tormentors had anticipated this strategy. They quietly continued to serve Carvajal the same food, intercepted the communications, and, once again, used the information in their favor. It should be noted that the inquisitors, like the Nazis centuries later, were known for their punctiliousness. Their record-keeping habits are an invaluable resource for those documenting their infamous history.

Their cunning in executing elaborate schemes isn't well known in Mexico outside the circles of historians and other specialists. The institution's chapter is seldom discussed in high schools and universities, for example. And it has seldom been written about in the country's poetry, novels, and theater—though, as we'll see, dissident artists have increasingly found inspiration in Carvajal. When the Inquisition does enter into curricula and discussion, it is in the context of the evangelization of the indigenous population. Bishop Juan de Zumárraga, the author of the first book ever printed in Mexico, is a recurring figure in these inquisitorial studies. But little is said about the persecution of crypto-Jews and other "deviants" by the Mexican branch of the Inquisition.

A prominent exception to the artistic silence around these issues can be found in the work of muralist Diego Rivera, who felt a close kinship with Carvajal. Rivera believed that his own family had Jewish ancestry. He dramatically portrays the plight of crypto-Jews in various paintings and murals, including an epic depiction of Carvajal's sister Mariana in the legendary *Sueño de una tarde dominical en la Alameda Central* (Dream of a Sunday afternoon in Alameda Park, 1946–47), currently on display at the Museo Diego Rivera in downtown Mexico City.[5] And Rivera's *Epopeya del pueblo mexicano* (Epic of the Mexican people, 1929–35), on a majestic staircase wall of Mexico's National Palace, features a fragment illustrating an auto-da-fé that is probably inspired by Carvajal's ordeal.

The fight to shape Carvajal's narrative for posterity began immediately upon his death. In a crowning passage, Cohen states that on the day after the auto-da-fé, a Dominican monk by the name of Fray Alonso de Contreras, whom Carvajal had designated as his confessor, took a deposition in which he averred that Carvajal "had undergone a sudden conversion in the last moments of his life, that he had confessed his sins and begged for reconciliation with the Church." Cohen pointedly adds that there were no other witnesses to this event.

No wonder Carvajal's journey is engaging. It is simultaneously about persecution and resistance, about freedom and survival.

In his journals, Søren Kierkegaard observes that "the tyrant dies and his rule is over, the martyr dies and his rule begins." The case of Luis de Carvajal the Younger is illustrative. His death finally brought his misery to an end, but other crypto-Jews heard about him and promoted his legacy. Although they didn't have direct access to his writings, they repeated stories about his ordeal. The myth grew. It traveled across centuries. It became a form of resistance, and Carvajal's quest—full of psychotic ups and downs—became his finest creation.

Cohen once told me that Carvajal's path is yet to be sufficiently understood, not only in the Hispanic world but in the Jewish world as well. His fight for self-determination resonates today because free spirits—e.g., fighters for freedom of conscience—continue to be oppressed. Although our world has felt the effects of progress, not much has changed when it comes to allowing people to express their own dissenting ideas and choose their own destiny.

Part II Found

*And whoever saves a life,
it is considered as if he
saved an entire world.*

—*Talmud Yerushalmi*
Sanhedrin 4:1 (22a)

The Chronicler

In 2016, early in the summer, I received an unexpected email from my old friend Esther "Starry" Schor, who teaches English at Princeton University and is the author of an award-winning biography of Emma Lazarus and a book on the development of Esperanto. I hadn't talked to Starry for some time. She said that a friend, Leonard Milberg—a Princeton alum and the donor of the Milberg Collection of Jewish American Writers—was interested in purchasing an item by Carvajal that had been recently put up for sale. She wanted to know if I would be willing to advise the collector about the potential purchase.

She embedded a link to the Swann Auction Galleries in Manhattan, which led to a description of the item: "Early transcript of Inquisition victim Luis de Carvajal's autobiographical *Memorias* with devotional manuscripts." It also stated, "The present volume clearly dates not long after Carvajal's lifetime." Surmising its historical relevance, I alerted Starry to the possibility of its being the stolen booklet. I described in some detail the theft that took place more than eighty years before. By this time, I had come to feel resigned about Carvajal's memoir, thinking it would never surface again. Despite its uncontested historical value, no one really seemed to care about its disappearance. As a Mexican, I have always felt that the country's mundane chaos contributes to the slow chipping away of its patrimony.

A few years before, with artist Steve Sheinkin, I had turned Carvajal into a character in a graphic novel, *El Iluminado* (2012). I had done this playfully, creating a thriller—with a nosy professor as a protagonist, whose name is Ilan Stavans—about

rival scholars connected with the loss of a historical manuscript. But apart from the drama, my real
goal was to attach Carvajal to the ebullient movement of crypto-Jewish awakening in the American
Southwest in the early twenty-first century. My
inspiration was Umberto Eco's medieval thriller
The Name of the Rose (1980), which was, at least
in part, inspired by the metafictional world of the
Argentine writer Jorge Luis Borges, one of my
favorite writers. My graphic novel was enthusias-
tically received. It brought me numerous letters,
Facebook messages, tweets, and other correspondence from crypto-Jews in northern Mexico and
the American Southwest.

Borges was on my mind when I wrote *El Iluminado*. The plot takes place in present-day Santa Fe,
and considerable aspects of the content resulted from
a series of trips I made to New Mexico, Arizona,
Nevada, and northern Mexico in the first decade of
this century. The graphic novel reflects my consum-
ing interest in the tribulations of the crypto-Jews. I
studied the construction of the Cathedral Basilica of

St. Francis of Assisi in downtown Santa Fe closely, especially an inscription—in Hebrew letters—of the Tetragrammaton on the entrance arch. Archbishop Jean-Baptiste Lamy, the historical figure Willa Cather drew on for *Death Comes for the Archbishop* (1927), plays a role in my novel as well. Lamy is the hinge that connects the Cathedral Basilica to a grouping of earlier religious buildings, at least one of which was funded in part with Jewish money. Santa Fe, the graphic novel argues, was a refuge for crypto-Jews eager to maintain the appearance of a New Christian life by donating funds to a Catholic church in order to deflect attention from their hidden practices. Archbishop Lamy was partially aware of this subterfuge.

It was during my Santa Fe trips that I reread the work of Carvajal. Haunted by the missing memoir, I fantasized about a rare booklet that travels from Mexico City to the American Southwest, ending up in the hands of devout crypto-Jews. My interest pushed me in countless directions. I had read with admiration Cohen's thoroughly researched

biography. In it, the blueprint of Carvajal's hardship is set out clearly: the biography looks at religious persecution in the New World as a method of centralized political control.

Cohen's contribution, it turns out, was only the tip of the iceberg. Carvajal has inspired operas, films, and a variety of fictional accounts, among other artistic manifestations. For instance, Arturo Ripstein, a prominent Mexican filmmaker of Jewish heritage whose career started when he was an assistant to Spanish director Luis Buñuel, made *El Santo Oficio* (1974), which was nominated for a Palme d'Or at the Cannes Film Festival. It is a period piece loosely based on the Carvajal family. But I've read novels about Carvajal that were composed as far away as Australia. And at the Harry Ransom Center in Austin, Texas, there is a Carvajal-related manuscript by Anita Brenner, one of the most noteworthy commentators on Mexican art in the twentieth century and the author of the seminal *Idols Behind Altars* (1929). Brenner, who studied under Franz Boas and enjoyed a close but contentious friendship with Diego Rivera, wrote for *The Nation* as well as for American Jewish publications. Her focus in the Carvajal manuscript isn't Carvajal himself but his mother and sister.

Soon after my exchange with Starry, I was having a conversation with Leonard Milberg himself. Milberg was then the chairman of Milberg Factors, a commercial finance company founded by his father in 1937. A tall, insistent, passionate man of 85, he is originally from Flatbush and graduated from Princeton and the Wharton School before launching a successful career. He is known for his private collections of Irish literature and early American documents, and, over the years, he has donated substantial amounts of money to Princeton to expand its Irish studies program.

Milberg has also funded exhibits on Jewish life in the early American Republic. His heightened interest in Jewish history has grown out of his dismay with the increasing anti-Semitism in the world today. As he told me during a lunch at the New-York Historical Society, "I hope this effort

educates people on the active role Jews played in shaping our society."

We were there because the veteran institution on Central Park West was preparing an exhibit called *The First Jewish Americans: Freedom and Culture in the New World*. The exhibit had started at Princeton and was moving to the New-York Historical Society. It was scheduled to be open to the public from October 2016 to March 2017, and it was sponsored in part by Milberg, who had also contributed items from his own collection to the exhibition.

The title, *The First Jewish Americans*, was intended to convey a double meaning: the first Jewish Americans weren't only from the United States but also from other parts of the Americas. The Carvajal booklet he hoped to acquire would serve as an example of Jewish life long before the American Revolution of 1776. But Milberg was not sure that the booklet would be ready for the show; he was involved with lawyers, scholars, and others trying to figure out whether it was authentic—and to ensure that his acquisition of it wouldn't violate any international laws.

Swann Auction Galleries had listed it for $50,000 to $75,000, but, again, the Swann described the manuscript as a transcription, not the original, dating it to "not long after Carvajal's lifetime." After Milberg had spotted it, he wanted to know whether I would recommend that he buy it. (In our discussions, Milberg endearingly pronounced Carvajal's name "Car-vee-dzal.") My feeling at first was that the manuscript might be a replica. Still, I suggested that Milberg cautiously proceed, in the unlikely case it was the original. I described to him the scholarly rivalry between del Toro and Nachbin and the disappearance of the booklet and the transcriptions. I also mentioned that, should this be the real thing, I assumed that the FBI should be brought in. And then I wondered out loud: what if the booklet were the genuine artifact? In that case, I told Milberg, he might be on the cusp of stirring up a hornet's nest. The ensuing outcry could bring about nothing short of an international scandal.

"My immediate reaction was that these books were too good to be true," Milberg would later state. "I surmised that they were either stolen or fake."

Within the next half hour, I shared the Swann Auction Galleries link with a series of colleagues in Mexico, the United States, and Australia whose interest in Carvajal had turned them into a kind of secret coterie. Some nurtured a hunch that the Carvajal memoir had finally reemerged. If that were the case, they thought any purchase of it in the United States would be unlawful, and they were eager to seek intervention by the Mexican government. Others were more skeptical, including my friend Santiago Cohen, an artist with whom I had recently collaborated and, like me, a Mexican Jew. He was in the middle of a graphic novel of his own on Carvajal.

Within a matter of days, Starry told me that Milberg had just learned from the Swann that "the Inquisition transcript was sold in London in December 2015 and brought 1,000 British pounds. The purchaser is the current seller." Starry added a bit later, "Where is Umberto Eco when you need him?" (Eco had died in Milan just a few months earlier.)

I reached out to my friend Barry Carr, a prominent Latin American historian and professor emeritus at La Trobe University in Melbourne, Australia. We had spoken at the PEN International Festival in April 2016, when Carr mentioned that a few months prior to the disappearance of the Carvajal booklet from the Archivo, an enigmatic scholar, possibly Brazilian, possibly a kleptomaniac, had stolen a precious treasure from the Mexican national archives. His last name, he said, was Nachbin. In our conversation, he imagined Nachbin to still be alive, which I have never been able to prove. "Definitely material here for a documentary, a novel, and maybe a film," Carr said to me.

With Carr as my Virgil, I soon found out that after the incident at the Archivo, Nachbin's whereabouts became increasingly difficult to pin down. By some accounts, he traveled to Brazil, where he founded and edited a Yiddish newspaper; others had him going to Spain, where he served as a newspaper correspondent assigned to various fronts of the Spanish Civil War until he was killed at one of them. And there were also rumors that he had returned to Europe and perished in the Holocaust. "You should write a *crónica*, Ilan," said Carr, referring to the long-narrative journalistic genre popular in Latin America. (In spite of Carr's help, I was never able to find what happened with the Carvajal booklet after 1932. I still don't know.)

When I shared the new details about the auction listing with him, Carr was ecstatic. He looked at the whole quest against a larger canvas. "I thought of this repatriation of Mexican *patrimonio* a few days ago as I was going through the mountains of correspondence accumulated since 1972," he said. "La Trobe University, where I taught between 1972 and 2007, at one point held a small but significant collection of pre-Columbian figurines, pottery, and other objects which it acquired (as a gift, I think) from a mining-company executive in Australia who had been a collector. I and my colleagues were not happy about the university's acceptance. I recall that we found a way to alert the Mexican authorities, via the Mexican embassy in Canberra, the Australian capital, about the existence of these objects. This was back in the early 1990s. . . . The end result was a correct institutional decision to return the materials to Mexico. I have a vivid memory of the little ceremony that was held at La Trobe when the official handover happened. We all felt 'good' after the episode."

Carr's next move was to consult with Anna Lanyon, a former doctoral student he had advised years before. Lanyon was an Australian novelist whose oeuvre often addressed Mexican topics, as in her *Fire and Song: The Story of Luis de Carvajal and the Mexican Inquisition* (2011), which is built as a fictionalized tale of Carvajal and his entourage. She had come across the story in 1994 while she gathered material for another book. "It was the kind of accidental encounter that often happens in archives," she wrote in the preface. "We may not find what we are looking for, but sometimes we find other treasures instead."[1]

"I just sent [Lanyon] a link to the auction site," Carr said to me, "and within fifteen minutes she called me, very excited. . . . She has copies of Luis Carvajal's handwriting and is also familiar with many of the Inquisition's scribes who prepared copies of Carvajal's diary and other documents. . . . [T]he 64,000-peso question is whether the item up for auction is one of the copies made by Inquisition scribes or the original. At first glance, Anna told me (on the phone) that it 'looked' like the handwriting of a scribe but she wasn't too sure and would need to get home and retrieve her copies of Carvajal's handwriting. So the mystery continues! What happened to the scholar Jacques Nachbin who allegedly removed/stole the original of the diary kept at the *Archivo* in Mexico City? What happened to him in Spain where he later went as a reporter for a Brazilian Jewish newspaper during the Spanish Civil War (he was never seen again)? Why is an Australian scholar interested? Definitely the stuff of novels!"

In a matter of days, at home with time to ponder, Lanyon wrote back again. The sudden appearance

of the documents meant a great deal to her. "I always felt that most of Luis's writing would turn up one day," she confided. "Luis wrote the original in tiny letters in a small black notebook measuring 9 × 15 centimeters (approx. 4 × 6 inches), while teaching at the Franciscan College of Santiago Tlatelolco between 1590 and 1595," she wrote. "The photo in the Swann catalogue shows margin notes of the sort the scribes customarily made, so I don't think this is the original. Also, it appears to be a full-size parchment." She added, "However, I feel certain that the other two, smaller manuscripts listed are in Luis's own hand. In February 1595, he gave the Holy Office informer, Luis Díaz, a tiny notebook in which he had copied out the Ten Commandments. The first letters in this book were illuminated, as are the ones in the third item shown in the catalogue. Díaz passed Luis's gift to the inquisitors. Their scribes would have copied the text of this notebook, but it is most unlikely that they would attempt to reproduce its miniature size or its illuminated letters, so the document in the catalogue is probably the original. (Luis had smuggled it into prison in the taffeta around the brim of his hat—that's how small it was.)"

Lanyon concluded, "The second item of the three listed is, I think, another of Luis's tiny devotional notebooks. On 9 February 1595, he instructed Díaz, on his release, to go to the house in Santiago Tlatelolco where the Carvajal family had been living, and retrieve two notebooks hidden there. Luis wanted Díaz to wrap them 'as if they were a parcel of letters' and send them to his brothers in Pisa. The inquisitors sent their constable to the house. He found one book—Luis's *memoria*—but not the other one. When I wrote my book about Luis de Carvajal, I suggested that one of Luis's sisters, or a friend, may have already removed it for safe-keeping. It seems possible it could be the second item in the Swann catalogue, although I have no idea how it came to be with the family in Michigan. Luis was a fine Latinist who spent the last five years of his life (prior to his second arrest) translating portions of the scriptures into Spanish for his family and friends, so the content of the two smaller catalogue items fit exactly with this kind of translation work. I'm sure they are his, and feel so excited about them, that I can hardly type these words!"

She made a point of emphasizing to me that, in her view, the items on sale were *not* the ones stolen by Nachbin, but that did not dampen her excitement. For her, the question was whether Carvajal's memoir and transcriptions should go back to the Archivo or to Princeton. "The Bancroft has the second trial transcripts of Leonor and Isabel de Carvajal, and also of Luis's great friend Manuel de Lucena. I believe the Bancroft bought them with the approval of the [Archivo]."

I put Lanyon in touch with Starry. And through Starry, I put Milberg in touch with Martin A. Cohen, author of *The Martyr*.

Cohen only infrequently talked publicly about his research. Still, I thought he needed to know right away about the possible discovery of the Carvajal booklet. He preferred phone to email, so

I called him. In our conversation, he reiterated to me a fact he had mentioned a number of times over the years: while doing research at the Archivo for *The Martyr*, he was sure he had held the Carvajal booklet in his hand. This is impossible, though. Cohen worked on his biography of Carvajal in the 1950s, a couple of decades after the del Toro–Nachbin feud. If his recollection was correct, then the booklet and transcriptions for sale at the Swann Auction Galleries were inauthentic.

Cohen never relented on this point, but I strongly believe that his recollection, as sharp as it is, is wrong. Memory is fragile by definition. Guy de Maupassant once said that "memory is more perfect than our universe: it gives life where life does not exist." What we remember is never the past; it is only a version of the past. Cohen probably browsed through a copy of Carvajal's manuscript—one was indeed made before 1932—which he came to remember as the original.

At any rate, I told him that the original Carvajal booklet, or at the very least a scribal copy, had been found. I asked whether I could have Milberg ring him. Cohen consented. He was excited to know that after decades of wandering, the most important text written by a crypto-Jew in the Americas had now reemerged. "It's been a kind of bondage," he said. "Like the wandering of the Israelites for forty years in the desert."

The Collector

The price of the Carvajal booklet at the Swann Auction Galleries was fifty times the amount it had sold for a few months earlier in London. Scholars had suggested that its value might be closer to $500,000, but the auction house wasn't sure about the manuscript's legitimacy. This doubt was probably behind the relatively low price.

In fact, Bloomsbury Auctions had listed the item as "three small devotional manuscripts." It didn't even mention the Carvajal connection. To Joseph Berger, the *New York Times* reporter who later wrote about the discovery of Carvajal's memoir, a manuscript staff member at Bloomsbury had said that the item had been "from the library of a Michigan family, and in their possession for several decades."

Much as I have tried, I haven't been able to trace the whereabouts of the Michigan family. The protocol in manuscript collecting rigorously protects the collector's privacy. The only clue that became available was that the London buyer was a rare-book dealer who put the Carvajal memoir and transcriptions up for sale at the Swann. But answers were in reach. Was this truly Carvajal's text, written in ink by his own hand? At this point, my understanding of the work's shape and provenance depended on reports from Milberg and others. The material would need to be authenticated by a proper manuscript specialist.

Then, within a relatively short time, the Swann's posting of the Carvajal booklet was removed.

Over the next several months, Milberg regularly updated me on the progress of the investigation. During that time, I traveled to South America and New Zealand. Meanwhile, the FBI was contacted. The case was eventually moved to the Office of the US Attorneys.

When I periodically returned to the United States, I reached out to the US Attorney. He told me that

Steve Ferguson, the librarian for rare books and special collections at Princeton, had informed him that the Archivo listed the three texts as "missing for 90 years." At Ferguson's prompting, Philadelphia bookdealer David M. Szewczyk as well as Ken Ward of the John Carter Brown Library, both of whom were experts on early Mexican material, had made the trip to the Swann to scrutinize the manuscripts. And after nearly a century of intrigue and frustration, the core question was finally definitively answered: the texts were Carvajal's original memoir along with transcriptions from his own hand. As Milberg later told Berger of the *New York Times*, "No transcriber would have bothered to make the handwriting so tiny." The newspaper also quoted Rick Stattler, a curator in the rare-books department at Swann Auction Galleries. When he realized that the booklet was Carvajal's original, Stattler said, "I actually had the hairs go up on my arms."

By now I had joined the chorus of those who believed that the booklet was authentic. I would not get to see the manuscript myself until mid-

December, when it was already at the New-York Historical Society. I arrived late. Milberg graciously gave me a special tour with the zeal of a proud owner, explaining in detail each of the items in the exhibit. He reiterated to me that when he finally saw Carvajal's booklet and other items in "their exquisite remarkable tiny script," he knew "they were real."

After the tour, we had lunch. I left exhilarated. At last the long-lost volume had been found, and it was time to return it to the Archivo. But Milberg's intention all along had been to acquire the auction items with the explicit purpose of showing them in the New-York Historical Society exhibit and then donating them to his alma mater. I recall recommending that he strike a deal with the Mexican government, one whereby he would buy the Carvajal material for Mexico but receive permission to copy the texts, include them in the New York show, and then repatriate them to Mexico. In fact, knowing Mexico as I do, I encouraged him to persuade the Mexican government to create a special place for their public exhibition so as to avoid any future thefts—and to donate the gift in honor of the Mexican Jewish community.

Milberg recalled his thinking somewhat differently in his speech at the opening of the New-York Historical Society exhibit: "I took solace in being a good citizen." He couldn't abide being "deeply disappointed" at "not being able to display these incredible, precious books, undoubtedly the most important Jewish objects of the New World at my exhibit." Thus, "I concocted a plan to enable the Carvajal work to be in view even if it cost me some money. . . . The return was to be in honor of Mexico's Jewish community. I also requested better security at the Archives."

He was probably right. In the end, it doesn't matter what sequence of events is correct. I didn't hold out much hope for the Jewish community in Mexico to take an interest in the Carvajal booklet. In a country of almost 125 million, this minority of between 40,000 and 50,000 Jews has only recently begun to explore its past, and that interest seldom reaches as far back as the colonial period. More often than not, historians of Mexican Judaism concentrate on the Ashkenazi and Ottoman immigrations of the late nineteenth and early twentieth centuries, and to a lesser degree the arrival of refugees from the Holocaust in the 1940s. I have found no mention of Luis de Carvajal the Younger in the textbooks assigned in Jewish schools today. Certainly, there were none when I was growing up in the 1970s.

Worse, I didn't see a reason why Mexico itself would be interested in using the Carvajal booklet to foster a thorough study of the colonial period through crypto-Jewish eyes. Although welcoming to Jewish immigrants, Mexico harbors deep anti-Semitic sentiments. These sentiments have never manifested themselves in explosive ways; the country's history doesn't include pogroms and other anti-Jewish outbursts. Yet Jews are constantly viewed with suspicion. You notice it in the press, where Holocaust denial occasionally pops up, not to mention a strong anti-Israeli fervor that spills over onto the Mexican Jewish community.

Only a handful of prominent Mexican historians are aware of the plight of Luis de Carvajal the Younger. The vast majority have never heard of him or of other secret Jews during the colonial period, and there is little interest in the history of the Inquisition in Mexico. A museum that used to display a few torture instruments is now closed. All of this made me think that after the news of a triumphant repatriation of the Carvajal booklet, the item would be quickly forgotten. And if security is lax, it could vanish again into thin air.

In the end, as the *New York Times* announced, Milberg paid $2,500 to the Swann Auction Galleries and $10,000 to the Swann's consignor. His agent, William Reese, received $25,000. And he arranged for three digital copies to be made before repatriation: one for Princeton, one for the New-York Historical Society, and one for Congregation Shearith Israel, the Spanish-Portuguese synagogue on West 70th Street, on Manhattan's Upper West Side.

As the case was wrapped up, Anna Lanyon told me she was thrilled that Carvajal's precious documents would go back to the Archivo. "He told the inquisitors that he wanted them to keep his testament in his trial transcript, as proof of his faith. I imagine he would have wanted the *memoria* to stay there too, for the same reason."

While in New Zealand, I was contacted by Mexico's Consul General in New York, Diego Gómez Pickering. His assistant stated that he had "expressed great interest in meeting you at your earliest convenience to learn more about your literary research. Would you be available to come to the Consulate next week at some point?" During my next visit to the city, I stopped by the consulate, on East 39th Street, roughly between the Morgan Library and the Chrysler Building. Consul Gómez Pickering thanked me for my role in advising Leonard Milberg and told me he was delighted that Carvajal's booklet was scheduled to be repatriated.

He had something else in mind. He wanted me to write a piece about the entire affair: "Mexico needs to be better known for what it has always

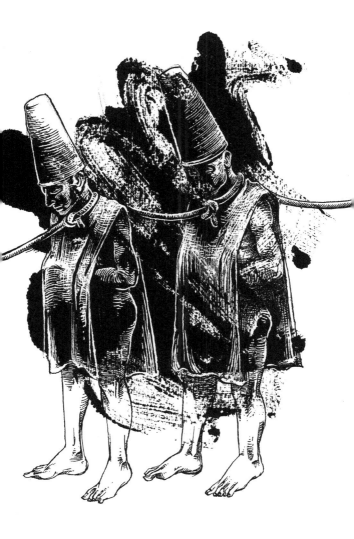

been: a place of tolerance and diversity. Jews play a critical role in that place."

I confess to having experienced an abrupt feeling of discomfort. For one thing, the relationship between the government and Mexican intellectuals is rife with tension. For Consul Gómez Pickering to suggest that I now praise the Mexican government for negotiating a beneficial deal, whereby an American Jewish philanthropist would return to Mexico what rightfully belongs to it, felt hypocritical. In other words, the last thing I wanted was to be told by him what to write.

Moreover, I still believe that the Mexican government had been and continues to be reckless when it comes to safeguarding the nation's cultural capital. While I was gratified that the Carvajal materials were being rightly returned to their original place, I was overtaken by a fear that lax oversight could put the artifacts at risk.

My concern was born out of experience. In the late 1980s, as I was working on my doctoral dissertation at Columbia University on detective fiction in Mexico, I spent long hours at the Archivo as well as at the Hemeroteca Nacional, the country's periodical depository. I was lucky to find a substantial amount of the material I was looking for, including first editions of novels. I found yellowed newspapers and magazines where the first instances of private-eye literature had been published. Yet I was shocked by the scant budget allocated to the Hemeroteca.

One especially shameful incident has never left my memory. I was after a particular review written by Borges in Buenos Aires in the late 1940s and published in a Saturday magazine. I looked for it in vain for hours. The staff assistant only allowed me to borrow four bound volumes at a time. At first she applauded my patience, but soon got annoyed by it, insinuating that Borges is a favorite author and that people steal his work when they find it. She said that I'd better focus on something else.

At some point I took a break to go to the men's room. The bathroom had no paper towels. And when I looked for toilet paper, I realized that there was none in the stalls. Shockingly, what I found instead were magazine pages folded and then cut into small squares. By chance, one of them had a tiny fragment of the Borges review I wanted.

I took it with me.

Since then I haven't been to either the Hemeroteca or the Archivo, in part for fear of experiencing firsthand that archival research in Mexico is still *en la Edad Media*. This is an expression in Mexican Spanish that refers to the country's exasperating bureaucracy. It is meant ironically, for Mexico, like all colonies, obviously never went through the Middle Ages.

Soon Milberg himself was also calling me. He echoed the Consul General's request: Would I write about it all? Milberg reminded me that in one of our many conversations, I had told him that this whole Purim spiel felt like a detective story, one with biblical underlayers, historical twists, and confounding semiotics.

Maybe I will write about it, I answered him. Before that, though, I thought I should call an acquaintance at the *Times*.

A few months later, I got another unexpected email. This time it was from Mexico: an invitation to attend the opening of the exhibit *The Return to Mexico: The Manuscript Carvajal*, scheduled to open on 4 April 2017, at the Museo Memoria y Tolerancia, part of Mexico City's downtown Centro Histórico.

The Museo opened its doors in October 2010. It is devoted to fighting discrimination of all sorts and bringing people's attention to genocidal movements that have decimated entire ethnic, religious, and cultural groups. The institution is part of an emerging trend in Latin America. For example, in Buenos Aires, Argentina, there is a memorial devoted to the *desaparecidos* and other victims of the Dirty War fought by the military junta in the 1970s against left-leaning groups. And in Santiago, Chile, a museum was built to remember those tortured and murdered by General Augusto Pinochet, who held power from 1973 to 1990.

The Mexican museum is more ecumenical. It has a section devoted to the Holocaust of six million

Jews by the Nazis during the Second World War. There are also halls commemorating genocides in Armenia, Rwanda, Bosnia, Guatemala, Cambodia, Darfur, and elsewhere. This list is at once encouraging and disheartening: it allows visitors to reflect on the effects of bigotry in the world, but does not take Mexico to account for having consistently ignored, and even massacred, its indigenous population. To focus attention on global disasters but not on local atrocities is hypocritical—an endorsement of silence.

To me, the act of placing the Carvajal booklet at the Museo Memoria y Tolerancia had all the trappings of a publicity stunt. The email I got came with a press release featuring statements from Baltazar Brito, director of the country's Biblioteca Nacional de Antropología e Historia. It announced that Leonard Milberg had given the artifact as a donation in honor of his friend Rafael Kalach, a member of the Mexican Jewish community.[1]

Carvajal's memoir belongs in an active, secure, special collection in a trustworthy library. It isn't simply an item to view; that can be done through photographs. It is an invaluable document that ought to be studied with care in order to understand what crypto-Jews endured during the campaign by the Inquisition to undermine Jewish beliefs. The Museo Memoria y Tolerancia is no research institution. And nowhere does it explore the plight of crypto-Jews as an example of intolerance.

I called Leonard Milberg. I told him that I had received an invitation to go to Mexico City for the opening at the Museo, although I probably wouldn't be able to attend. He mentioned that the Mexican government was thinking of bestowing on him the Aztec Eagle, the highest honor given to foreigners.

I smiled. Although the return of the lost Carvajal booklet appeared altogether accidental, I sensed a deeper meaning to the entire odyssey. It seemed to me that the attempt to look, with objective eyes, at the first Jews in the Americas was a corrective in *American* history—that is, not only for the United States but for the other Americas as well. This signified that Jewish life south of the Rio Grande, generally ignored by historians, was coming into focus.

Indeed, it seemed to me that the growth of the Latino minority in the United States had indirectly pushed the stolen manuscript out of obscurity. Even if I had some doubts, for an American Jew to purchase an artifact about the Spanish Inquisition and the plight of persecuted crypto-Jews and then rightfully return the item to its original place in Mexico, but not before the whole story made international news, was a corrective. It was a statement that Jews in the New World have deep roots, and that those roots need to be studied and integrated into Mexican and American history.

"Mazel tov!" I said. "Car-vee-dzal would be laughing."

"Why?" Milberg asked.

"The very same country that burned him at the stake is now celebrating his triumphant return. It is nothing but ironic."[2]

Notes

1. According to one historian, the encounter between Europe and the pre-Columbian people of what would one day be known as the Americas is "the meeting of two dreams. There is the Spanish dream of gold, a devouring, pitiless dream, which sometimes reached the heights of cruelty; it was an absolute dream, as if there were something at stake entirely different from the acquisition of wealth and power; a regeneration in violence and blood to live the myth of Eldorado, when everything would be eternally new. The other side was the ancient dream of the Mexicans, a long-awaited dream, when from the east, from the other side of the ocean, those bearded men guided by the Feathered Serpent Quetzalcóatl would come to rule over them once again. Thus, when the two dreams and the two peoples met, the one demanded gold

and riches, whereas the other wanted only a helmet to show to the high priests and the kings of Mexico, since, as the Indians said, it resembled those once worn by their ancestors, before they disappeared. Cortés gave them a helmet, but demanded that it be brought back to him filled with gold. When Montezuma saw the helmet, Bernal Díaz tells us, 'he was more than ever convinced that we were the people spoken of by his ancestors as coming to rule his land.'" Jean-Marie Gustave Le Clézio, *The Mexican Dream: or, The Interrupted Thought of Amerindian Civilizations*, trans. Teresa Lavender Fagan (Chicago: University of Chicago Press, 1965; repr., 1993), 2–3.

2. In Spanish, *lumbroso* is a malapropism derived from the noun *lumbre*, meaning light, glow, splendor. It explains why Carvajal nicknamed himself "El Iluminado" (The Enlightened).

3. As one historical summation puts it, "The Holy Office has a venerable reputation as a juggernaut of death, based as it happens largely on fiction. . . . Taking into account all the tribunals of Spain up to about 1520, it is unlikely that

more than two thousand people were executed for heresy in that period by the Inquisition. Very few were executed in the next three centuries, and we can in all probability accept the estimate, made on the basis of available documentation, that a maximum of three thousand persons may have suffered death during the entire history of the tribunal. Figures for executions do not of course tell the whole history of cruelty and oppression, since the negative impact of the Holy Office extended far beyond the question of burnings." Henry Kamen, *The Spanish Inquisition: A Historical Revision*, 4th ed. (New Haven: Yale University Press, 2014), 252.

4. Kamen writes about the move to embrace Catholicism in Spain: "Who were the conversos? At the upper social level, they played a significant role in some towns of Castile and the crown of Aragon. By changing their religion after 1391, successful Jewish families became qualified to hold public office in the towns, with a consequent growth of rivalry between newcomers and the older oligarchies. . . . The political role of conversos was evidently limited

only to a handful of towns where Jews had been numerous, but in those few it could be significant" (ibid., 36). In a footnote, Kamen notes that there is a vast, often polemical, literature on the subject and that some scholars prefer the term *crypto-Jew* to *converso*, which, he states, "presupposes (incorrectly) that the person was always a secret Jew." The nomenclature is indeed muddled. Benzion Netanyahu (the father of Israeli politician Benjamin Netanyahu), in his mammoth volume *The Origins of the Inquisition in Fifteenth-Century Spain* (New York: Random House, 1995), uses the terms *conversos*, *Marranos*, and *New Christians* synonymously, justifying the approach by arguing that "each of them has long served to designate the same group in Jewish, Spanish, and European scholarship." In my own use, a *New Christian* is the same as a *converso*, in that Judaism has been completely rejected in favor of Christianity, where a *crypto-Jew* retains private loyalty to the Jewish faith. It isn't that simple, though. At times, a descendant of New Christians would rediscover the old religious identity, thus becoming a crypto-Jew.

5. This is, obviously, a cruel irony, given that the Carvajal saga is nothing if not an exposé of Hispanic anti-Semitism. As one historian acutely describes the Spanish Inquisition, it was "a new type of anti-Semitism—one that held Jewish blood to be a hereditary taint that could not be eradicated by baptism. This was the origin of Spanish racism, the first of its kind in Europe to be specifically directed against the *mala sangre* (bad blood) of the Jews and to become fixated on the issue of *limpieza de sangre* (blood purity)." Robert S. Wistrich, *A Lethal Obsession: Anti-Semitism from Antiquity to the Global Jihad* (New York: Random House, 2010), 93.

CHAPTER 2

1. Mexican historian Edmundo O'Gorman (1906–1995), author of *The Invention of America* (1958), wrote that "New Spain is a period in which a nun's spiritual flight, a terminally-ill person's miraculous cure, a sinner's repentance, or a whole woman's vaticinations [prophecies] are more important news than the rise in prices

in business or the imposition of a sales tax; a period in which a spiritual journey to the interior of the soul is more momentous than the expeditions to California and the Philippines. . . . The historian who ignores this hierarchy of period values, might offer us an exhaustive and well-documented narrative of the historical events, but he will never penetrate the secret interior of the most significant events." Quoted in Francisco de la Maza, *Catarina de San Juan* (Mexico: Cien de México, 1970; repr., 1999), 58.

2. I contributed an introduction to the reprint: Martin A. Cohen, *The Martyr: Luis Carvajal, a Secret Jew in Sixteenth-Century Mexico* (Albuquerque: University of New Mexico Press, 2001).

3. Out of caution, Cohen doesn't use the term *schizophrenia* or any other similar psychiatric term. Yet he not only painstakingly narrates Carvajal's dreamlike life (to distinguish him from his uncle, he refers to him as "Luis") in ways that suggest, to me, bipolar disorder, but also describes the internal voices he heard. Self-anointed prophets usually follow this path of

hallucinatory persuasion. When Cohen analyzes the stringent regulations that governed every step of the procedures used by the Inquisition, from the gathering of evidence against a suspect to the final disposition of his case, he quotes from the *Autobiography*: "One night when he lay down to sleep, weary and depressed after a day when he had managed to fast and pray, Luis heard a voice in his dreams telling him to 'be strong and consoled, for the holy Job and Jeremiah are praying most efficaciously for you.' Buoyed by this dream, he was prepared psychologically for the dream that came to him several nights later. He called it a 'divine and true revelation,' for it assured him in the clearest terms that God had chosen him, like a prophet, for a high and lofty purpose in life. In this dream, suggested by the call of the biblical prophets, Luis saw a glass vial that was covered with a cloth, tightly stopped, and full of a precious liquid. The liquid was the elixir of divine wisdom, dispensed only in drops and only to the chosen few. Near the vial stood King Solomon, the Bible's paragon of wisdom, and not far away stood God. Luis heard God instructing Solomon to 'take a spoon and fill it with this liquid and give it to this boy to drink.' Solomon immediately executed the command and placed in Luis's mouth the spoonful of wisdom, with its delightful sweet taste. No sooner had he imbibed it, Luis recalled, than he felt consoled." Cohen, *Martyr*, 167.

4. In the Nahua language, *chichimeca* is the equivalent of "barbaric." According to Cohen, "They belonged to scores of different tribes, most of them primitive and savage" (ibid., 48). Cohen also quotes Miles Philips's *Relación*, which claims the Chichimecas "use [*sic*] to wear their hair long, even down to the knees. They do also color their faces green, yellow, red, and blue, which maketh them to seem very ugly and terrible to behold." See Joaquín García Icazbalceta, ed., *Obras*, vol. 7 (1898; repr., 1968), 151–296.

5. I explore the serpentine quest for an elusive Jewish ancestry of Diego Rivera and Frida Kahlo—who took different paths to arrive at similar conclusions—in the chapter "Kahlo's

Eyebrows" of my book *The Seventh Heaven: Travels Through Jewish Latin America* (Pittsburgh: University of Pittsburgh Press, 2019).

CHAPTER 3

1. Lanyon reproduces, in actual size, a page of Carvajal's *Autobiography*. In the bibliography, she offers a menu of the manuscripts related to the Carvajal trials that are held at the Archivo. She lists items on Luis de Carvajal y de la Cueva, Governor of Nuevo León (Inquisition vol. 11, exp. 3, Colección Riva Palacios, years 1589–90), on Luis de Carvajal, alias Joseph Lumbroso (Inquisition vol. 11, exp. 2, Colección Riva Palacios, first trial, years 1589–90, and second trial, years 1595–96), and on relatives Francisca Nuñes de Carvajal, Gaspar de Carvajal, Isabel de Andrada de Carvajal, Leonor de Andrada de Carvajal, Mariana Nuñez de Carvajal, and Baltasar Rodríguez de Carvajal. See Anna Lanyon, *Fire and Song: The Story of Luis de Carvajal and the Mexican Inquisition* (New South Wales: Allen and Unwin, 2011), 290, 291.

CHAPTER 4

1. Berger quotes Milberg as saying that highlighting an object like the Carvajal booklet was his way of "getting back at anti-Semitism." Milberg added, "I wanted to show that Jews were part of the fabric of life in the New World. This book was written before the Pilgrims arrived." Joseph Berger, "A Jewish Exodus to a New Nation," *New York Times*, 27 October 2016.

2. The chase isn't over altogether. On 26 October 2018, Leonard Milberg copied me on an email to Stephen Ferguson of Princeton about a couple of emails he had received: "The first e-mail has a link to a zip file with copies of documents that are owned by a Mexican couple living in New York and Mexico who approached me offering to sell them. The woman, Beatriz Mendivil, approached me and alleges that they have been in her husband's family for many years. She claims that the handwriting is our deceased friend Luis de Carvajal. The second e-mail contains papers which Ms. Mendivil claims are from [the] Mexican government referencing the documents and, according to

Ms. Mendivil, prove they were not stolen from the Mexican archives." Milberg asked Ferguson to forward the copies to the Mexican experts for analysis. He added, "Let's hope they are worthy of purchasing and they add a little knowledge about our deceased martyr friend Mr. Carvajal and that the price is reasonable."

The images by Eko in *The Return of Carvajal* are tailored etchings in copper plates. To convey the Manichean worldview of the Spanish Inquisition, an eighteenth-century technique that employs aquatint sugar lift for black brushstrokes is used. The sugar lift itself is a mixture of sugar and Chinese ink that is applied with a brush on a plate previously coated in bitumen-of-Judea resin adhered by heat. As the strokes dry out, the copper plate is covered in etching varnish and dipped in warm water. The process dissolves the sugar and ink mix. The plate is then submerged in a bath of iron perchloride or acid.